EGG to FROG

By Rachel Tonkin

Illustrated by Stephanie Fizer Coleman

CRABTREE
PUBLISHING COMPANY
WWW.CRABTREEBOOKS.COM

CRABTREE
PUBLISHING COMPANY
WWW.CRABTREEBOOKS.COM

Published in Canada
Crabtree Publishing
616 Welland Avenue
St. Catharines, ON
L2M 5V6

Published in the United States
Crabtree Publishing
PMB 59051
350 Fifth Ave, 59th Floor
New York, NY 10118

Published in 2020 by Crabtree Publishing Company

First published in Great Britain in 2019 by Wayland
Copyright © Hodder and Stoughton, 2019

Author: Rachel Tonkin

Illustrator: Stephanie Fizer Coleman

Editorial director: Kathy Middleton

Editors: Melanie Palmer, Janine Deschenes

Proofreader: Melissa Boyce

Designer: Lisa Peacock

Prepress technician: Samara Parent

Print coordinator: Katherine Berti

Videos by shutterstock

Printed in the U.S.A./072019/CG20190501

Library and Archives Canada Cataloguing in Publication

Title: Egg to frog / Rachel Tonkin and [illustrated by] Stephanie Fizer Coleman.
Names: Tonkin, Rachel (Children's author), author. | Coleman, Stephanie Fizer, illustrator.
Description: Series statement: Follow the life cycle | Includes index.
Identifiers: Canadiana (print) 20190092777 |
  Canadiana (ebook) 20190092785
  ISBN 9780778763864 (hardcover)
  ISBN 9780778763970 (softcover)
  ISBN 9781427123558 (HTML)
Subjects: LCSH: Frogs—Life cycles—Juvenile literature. |
  LCSH: Frogs—Metamorphosis—Juvenile literature. |
  LCSH: Tadpoles—Juvenile literature.
Classification: LCC QL668.E2 T66 2019 | DDC j597.8/9—dc23

Library of Congress Cataloging-in-Publication Data

CIP available at the Library of Congress

LCCN: 2019025343

CONTENTS

Hi, I'm Ava and this is Finn. Get ready for an inside look at nature's life cycles!

After reading this book, join us online at Crabtree Plus to learn more and enjoy some fun activities.

When you see a QR code, scan it with your device to see videos that make the life cycle come to life.

If your device does not have a built-in QR code reader, you must download an app.

Laying eggs

In spring, a female frog lays many eggs. She lays them in water, such as a pond. The eggs are soft. They stick together in a clump. The clump is called **frogspawn**.

Inside the eggs

The frogspawn floats
on the **surface** of the water.
Inside each egg, a baby
frog is growing. Each
egg is kept safe in
a ball of jelly.

Hatching

A baby frog is called a tadpole. After about one to three weeks, the tadpole **hatches** from its egg. It lives underwater.

Watch these tadpoles swim in a pond.

Tadpole

The young tadpole has a head and tail. It breathes through **gills** on the side of its head. It eats tiny plants and **algae** in the water.

Back legs

When the tadpole is about seven weeks old, its back legs begin to grow. Its tail begins to shrink. It starts to grow **lungs**. As it grows lungs, its gills tuck inside its skin.

This tiny
tadpole
has grown
back legs.

Front legs

After nine weeks, the tadpole grows front legs. It now uses lungs inside its body to breathe. It comes to the surface of the water to get air.

Froglet

After about 12 weeks, the tadpole becomes a young frog. A young frog is called a froglet. It can live on land and in water. Its tail is shrinking. Soon, it will have no tail.

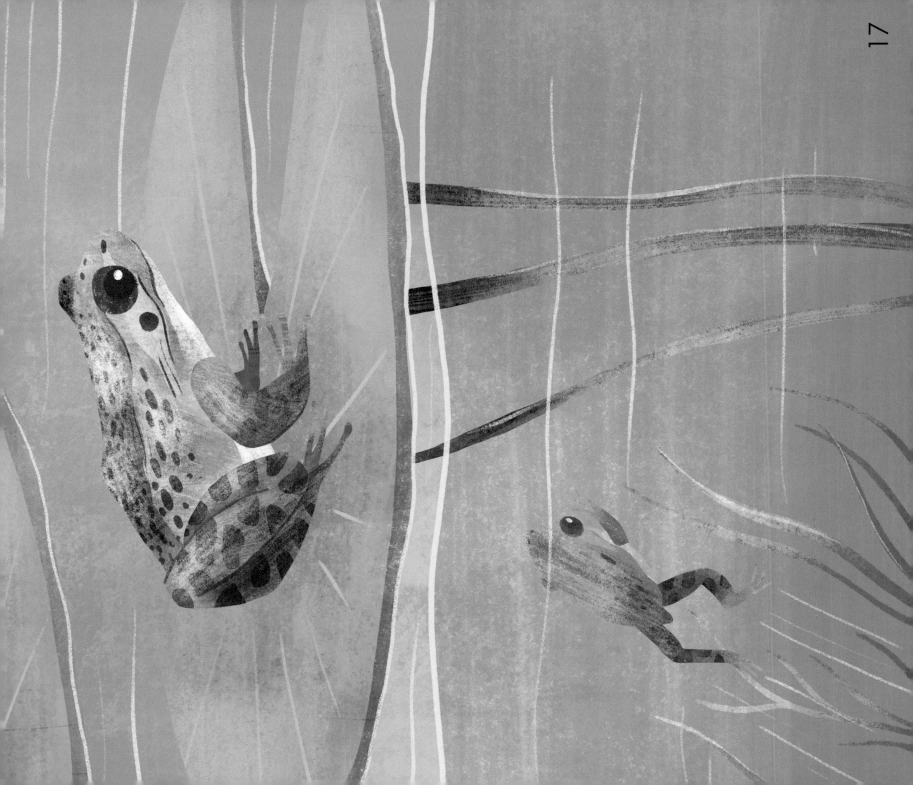

Adult frog

By fall, the froglet becomes an adult frog. It eats insects, worms, and slugs to help it grow. In winter, the frog **hibernates** at the bottom of a pond.

Mating

In spring, the frog finds another frog to **mate** with. The female frog now lays many eggs of her own. The **life cycle** starts again.

Listen to the sound frogs make when it is time to mate.

Frog life cycle

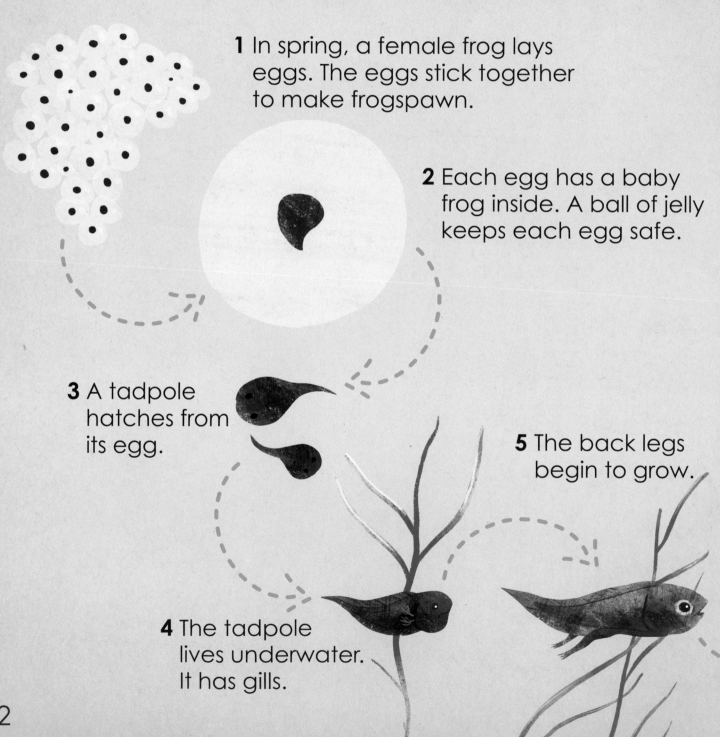

1 In spring, a female frog lays eggs. The eggs stick together to make frogspawn.

2 Each egg has a baby frog inside. A ball of jelly keeps each egg safe.

3 A tadpole hatches from its egg.

4 The tadpole lives underwater. It has gills.

5 The back legs begin to grow.

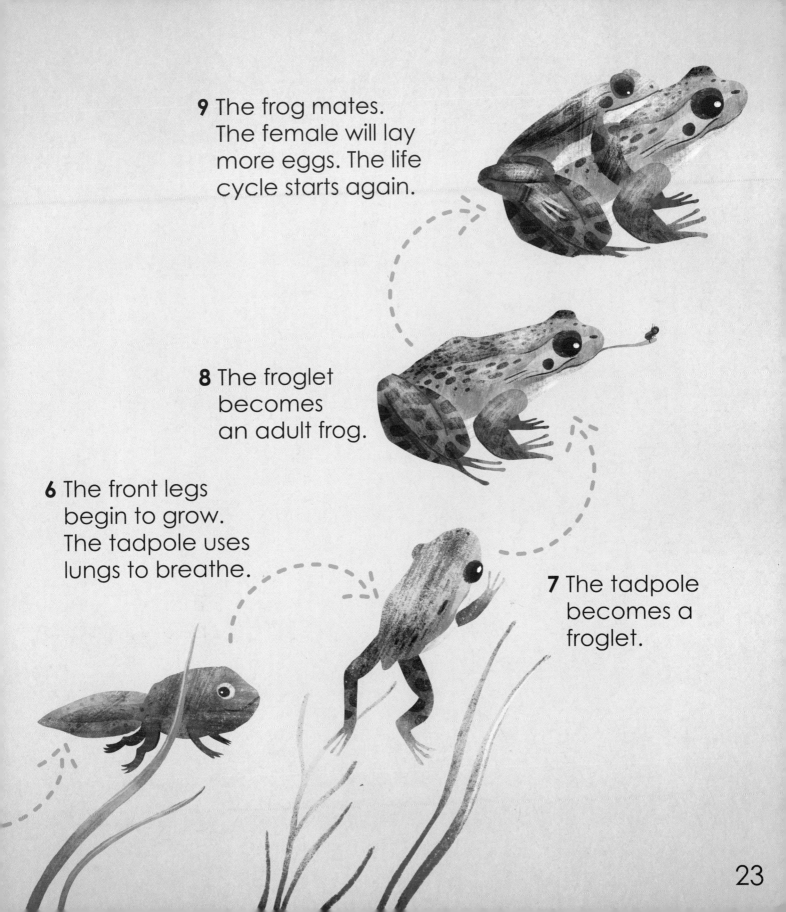

9 The frog mates. The female will lay more eggs. The life cycle starts again.

8 The froglet becomes an adult frog.

6 The front legs begin to grow. The tadpole uses lungs to breathe.

7 The tadpole becomes a froglet.

Words to know

algae Plants or plantlike living things that grow mostly in water

frogspawn A group of frog eggs that are stuck together and surrounded by jelly

gills An organ that allows fish to get oxygen from the water. Oxygen is the gas needed to breathe.

hatches Comes out of an egg

hibernates Sleeps or is not active during the winter

life cycle The stages a living thing passes through as it grows to adulthood

lungs The organs in the chest that allow humans and many other animals to breathe

mate When a male and female frog make baby frogs

surface The outside or top layer of something

Index

To explore and learn more, enter the code at the Crabtree Plus website below.

www.crabtreeplus.com/follow-the-life-cycle

Your code is:
flc15